GUNSMITHING MANUAL FOR NOVICES

A BEGINNER'S GUIDE TO THE TRADE OF GUNSMITHING FROM THE SCRATCH

JACK FERELL

Table of Contents

CHAPTER ONE

GUNSMITHING

Learning the Trade of Gunsmithing

Gunsmiths build, repair, and customise firearms such as handguns, rifles, and shotguns, as well as rifle and shotgun accessories. Disassembling, cleaning, inspecting, and reassembling a gun are some of the more basic tasks these gunsmiths can perform, but they are also capable of more complex work, such as refinishing metal, engraving designs into wood, and designing custom firearms.

Gunsmiths' work necessitates a wide range of expertise and knowledge. Gunsmiths need to be familiar with a wide range of firearms in order to design and modify weapons with custom parts and enhance their performance. Metalworking and metal finishing necessitates a thorough understanding of chemistry. There are some gunsmiths who use computer-aided design software in addition to blueprint reading. There are many other skills needed by gunsmiths, including welding and machining.

To become a gunsmith, what kind of education is required?

It is possible to become a gunsmith through apprenticeships, military training and a degree or certificate program, among others. Gunsmithing certificate and associate degree programs are available at a few select colleges and universities across the country, and enrolling in one of these programs is the best way to learn the trade.

Under the guidance of experienced instructors, students in gunsmith training programs learn about firearms safety, machine shop safety, firearms repair, stockmaking, and firearms conversion. Welding, metal finishing, gun blueing, and working with complicated machine tools are all highly valued.. Skills Students who enroll in a gunsmithing program will have plenty of opportunities to put their newly acquired skills to the test with the help of the school's tools and firearms. Gunsmith programs teach management skills as well, in case students decide to go into business for themselves.

In order to earn an associate degree in gunsmithing, students must complete two years of full-time study and take courses in English, mathematics, and science. Students who want to earn a certificate rather than an associate degree can do so by attending a school that offers both. Short-term or summer schools teaching basic skills are also offered in collaboration with the National Rifle Association by some schools.

How do I know if I need to be certified or licensed?

A federal firearms license, or FFL, is required for gunsmiths who work for a company. The Bureau of Alcohol, Tobacco, Firearms, and Explosives (ATF) issues FFLs (ATF). A gunsmith's application for a Federal Firearms License (FFL) must include a copy of their fingerprints and a fee. The applicant will be interviewed in person at the local ATF field office after their fingerprints have been submitted to the ATF for a criminal history background check.

The ATF has set bookkeeping standards for FFLs. Customers who leave their firearms with a gunsmith overnight must have their firearms recorded in a "bound book" for these purposes.

CHAPTER TWO

How long does it take to become a firearms repairman?

Obtaining an associate degree or certificate in gunsmithing can be completed in as little as two years, but many gunsmiths take several years of practice before they can open their own businesses.

For those who have served in the military or are machinists, the amount of time it takes to become a gunsmith can be significantly increased.

How much money does a gunsmith earn?

Gunsmiths in the United States make an average of $14 an hour, according to PayScale.com. Because of their passion for the craft, many people choose to pursue a career as a gunsmith despite its low pay.

Entrepreneurial gunsmiths also have to factor in the costs of running a business, such as purchasing tools and equipment, leasing space, paying taxes and employing staff. One's business salary is affected by all of these factors.

What are the prospects for finding a job?

Gunsmiths in the United States face an uncertain job market. Gunsmiths may see a decrease in demand in the future. Many gun manufacturers are making more affordable firearms with more customization options, such as the Glock 17 and Glock 19.

Other factors, on the other hand, suggest that the demand for gunsmiths will increase in the coming years. Data from FBI background check applications show that gun sales have been increasing at a rapid pace over the past few years. Increased gun sales have prompted manufacturers to hire more workers to meet demand, and this could lead to a rise in demand for independent gunsmiths as well.

After completing their training, new gunsmiths may begin working under the guidance of more seasoned gunsmiths. A gunsmith's career can take them from entry-level work to running their own shop, depending on their level of experience and education.

Gun manufacturers, sporting goods stores and independent

gunsmiths are all places where you can find work as a new gunsmith. Gunsmiths.com, for example, has a job board for gunsmiths. It's possible to network and learn about local job openings by attending conferences and career fairs.

In what ways can I expand my knowledge of gunsmithing?

Discussions about guns and gunsmithing can be found in a variety of forums on the Internet these days. Gunsmith enthusiasts and professionals can connect on these discussion boards to find out about each other's backgrounds in education, training, and employment. Those interested in pursuing a career as a gunsmith can find assistance from organizations such as the National Rifle Association and the American Gunsmithing Institute.

What are the advantages and disadvantages of becoming a gunsmith?

Gunsmiths are required for the manufacture of firearms. Gunsmiths are those who make or repair firearms, either from scratch or with the assistance of other gunsmiths. Considering the number of people who own guns, this is a necessity. You must be dedicated and meticulous in your work; you must also be able to operate machinery.

Being a gunsmith, on the other hand, has its advantages and disadvantages, just like any other profession. As a result, it's imperative that you fully understand what the job entails before signing up. As a result, we'll look at the pros and cons of working in this field. What are we waiting for?

You Have the Potential to Make a Significant Amount of Money

Working with firearms can be hazardous. A mishap can happen at any time. As a result, you should be compensated accordingly. The starting salary isn't the best, but it can rise over time.

An annual salary of $31,910 is the average for a gunsmith across the country. Compared to other professions, it's a pittance, but the good news is that it has the potential to rise over time. Practice as much as possible to earn more money. Working as an apprentice in a machine shop or for a gun manufacturer is mandatory for a period of time.

According to where they live, gunsmiths in the United States can earn more money than the national average wage. As an illustration, a gunsmith in New

York can earn up to $85,000 a year, while those in Texas, Pennsylvania, and Montana can expect to make anywhere from $61,000 to $79,000.

2. Attending University isn't Required.

An added perk of working as a gunsmith is that you are not required to go to college to pursue this career path. High school diploma is the minimum requirement, so you can begin working sooner and save three to four years of college time.

Of course, you can also pursue a career as a gunsmith by enrolling in a gunsmithing program. The job is more accessible, however, because it does not necessitate a college degree.

You'll Have to Deal with a Wide Range of Weapons.

The most exciting aspect of this job is, of course, the opportunity to use firearms. As a weapon enthusiast, you'll be a good fit in the field of work here. For starters, you'll be able to create them. As a result, you'll have to deal with a lot of different models, either repairing or redesigning them.

For example, better ergonomics, such as a good foregrip, may be required for some of them. The Bravo Company KeyMod Gunfighter KAG Angled Grip is an example of such a foregrip. It has a stop so that you can pull your rifle up to your shoulder with ease. It's small, angled, and doesn't take up much room on the handguard. Considering these benefits, it's easy to see why ergonomics would benefit from improvement.

CHAPTER THREE

4. Self-Expression

When it comes to gunsmithing, you have the freedom to express yourself. Designing guns can be an excellent way to express yourself if you've got a flair for the creative.

You'll be able to express your unique perspective on guns and your sense of humor in a way that no one else will be able to. It can be a lot of fun, and it gives you the opportunity to create something original.

People's safety can be improved by you.

In order to work as a gunsmith, you must first receive training in firearms instruction so that you can better protect your customers. As a result, you'll be helping to make the world a safer place by instructing others on how to keep themselves and their loved ones safe. Doing what's right gives you a sense of fulfillment.

Cons

Exposure to Firearms Residue.

Exposure to gunpowder residue is a drawback of this line of work. When it comes to your health, the residue can pose a risk. If you're working on a gun that has been used frequently, the risk of lead dust exposure is greater. As a result, it may pose a risk to you.

Not to mention that if you spend a lot of time with your family after work, you may be putting them at risk as well. For example, if you have children, you run the risk of putting them in danger as well.

Injuries caused by machinery are also a concern.

Gunsmithing does not necessitate the use of one's hands to carry out the work. It is necessary to have specific machinery on hand in order to construct and repair weapons. While this machinery can be used, you must first learn how to operate it. Using these machines incorrectly can result in serious injury.

Before using machinery like milling machines or grinders, you should receive instruction on how to use it safely. To top it all off, these machines come with a long list of rules that you must adhere to.

3. Weapons-Related Injury and Death Risks

Dealing with the actual weapons carries a significant amount of risk as well. Making or repairing guns can be dangerous because of the risk of accidentally firing them and injuring yourself or someone else. A major risk that you should be aware of and try to avoid at all costs.

Make sure the weapon isn't loaded when using it to avoid this. If you don't, you put yourself and others in danger.

The End of the Road

Before setting out on a journey, it's critical to weigh the advantages and disadvantages of each option. You should be aware of the downsides of becoming a gunsmith before you accept the position, which has its advantages and disadvantages. To the best of my ability, I hope this article gave you an idea of what it takes to be a gunsmith.

THE END

* 9 7 9 8 8 4 7 3 3 9 4 6 9 *